This book is dedicated to Henning and Anna,
two very special people whom I love!

With thanks to the expertise of Bob Hart,
USGS hydrologist and wild explorer of the hinterlands;
and to Caroline, who makes my words and paintings sing!

Chariot Victor Publishing
Cook Communications, Colorado Springs, CO 80918
Cook Communications, Paris, Ontario
Kingsway Communications, Eastbourne, England

OCEANS AND RIVERS
© 1999 by Michael Carroll

ISBN 0-78143-068-2
Designed by Andrea Boven
First printing, 1999
Printed in Singapore
03 02 01 00 99   5 4 3 2 1

Paintings by Michael Carroll
Photo Credits:
p. 3, 31 Waterfall (Michael Carroll)
p. 5, 27 Earth photo courtesy of NASA
p. 5, 21 Waterfall in Iceland (Michael Carroll)
p. 5 Antarctica (Dale Anderson)
p. 5, 30 Bad water in Death Valley (Michael Carroll)
p. 5, 9 Waves (Bill Gerrish)
p. 5, 11 Creatures (Bill Gerrish)
p. 12 Sea of Galilee (Duane Cory)
p. 12 Shore of the Mediterranean Sea (Duane Cory)
p. 14, 30 Hoover Dam (Michael Carroll)
p. 15, 30 Small rivers Michael Carroll)
p. 16 Jordan River (Duane Cory)
p. 17 Dry river bed (Duane Cory)
p. 26 Solar One power station (Michael Carroll)
p. 29 Patmos (C.D. Walt Burchett)
p. 31 Surf on the beach (Michael Carroll)

OCEANS AND
RIVERS

Michael Carroll

Chariot Victor Publishing
A Division of Cook Communications

OCEANS, SEAS, LAKES, AND RIVERS

The sea is his, for he made it, and his hands formed the dry land. Psalm 95:5

When astronauts look down on the Earth from space, they see mostly water. God has covered nearly three-fourths of the world in oceans, seas, lakes, and rivers. Most of the Earth's water is in its oceans. In fact, if you could put every drop of Earth's water into ten giant swimming pools, 9 1/2 of them would be water from the oceans.

An *ocean* is a giant body of water. There are four oceans on Earth: the Arctic, the Indian, the Atlantic, and the Pacific. Smaller bodies of water are called *seas*, and even smaller ones are called *lakes*. Some lakes are made when people build a dam to save water. Some lakes are made by underground rivers, called *springs*. Streams flow from lakes, making beautiful waterfalls as they splash down the mountains. The streams turn into rivers that pour into the seas and oceans.

Rivers, lakes, and seas gave people of ancient times good things to eat, salt for preserving food, and places to wash their clothes. Waterways helped people travel to distant places using boats and rafts.

Sailing on the open sea was another matter. To people of Bible times, the sea was mysterious and dangerous. There were unknown sea monsters and terrifying storms, and their boats were not strong. They knew there was a powerful God Who made the crashing seas.

Left **God has put many wonderful creatures in the sea. Some live near the air, while others spend their lives in the deep, dark depths.**

FUN FACTS

Largest Ocean: The Pacific stretches from North and South America to Asia and Australia, and covers nearly as much area as seven North American continents put together!

Deepest Place: The Marianas Trench in the Pacific Ocean is deeper than the highest mountain turned upside down.

Highest storm waves: Waves have been reported to be as tall as a ten-story building (111 feet)

Biggest Ocean Current: The Antarctic Circumpolar Current is an undersea river that carries 2,000 times more water than the biggest river in the world.

HOW THE OCEANS WORK

All streams flow into the sea, yet the sea is never full. To the place the streams come from, there they return again.

Ecclesiastes 1:7

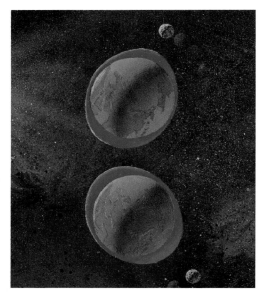

Above **Tides are caused by a bump in the ocean which is pulled out by the Moon.**

All bodies of water are made up of seawater or fresh water. Seawater is full of salt and minerals. Drinking seawater will make you sick. But even though we can't drink it, seawater has all sorts of minerals we can use. Fresh water is not salty, and it is what people need to live. This is the water we find in lakes and rivers, as well as out of the faucet in your kitchen.

Where does a lake or river get its fresh water? When the sun beats down on the Earth, water turns into vapor, or steam. It rises into the air, leaving behind the salt and minerals. Water vapor becomes clouds. When the air is just right, the vapor in the clouds turns back into water and falls as rain or snow. Some of the rain or melted snow soaks into the ground and some runs into lakes and rivers. The rivers run down the hills and mountains and across the plains, and they finally pour back into the ocean to start all over again. God's plan for recycling the Earth's water is called the *water cycle*.

The seas rise and fall each day. This rising and falling is called *tides*. Tides are caused by the pull of the Moon and the turning of the Earth. As the Moon goes around the Earth and the Earth spins, the pull of the Moon on the world's oceans causes a big bulge in the water. This bulge sloshes around the Earth much like water in a bowl that you hold when you walk. The ocean seems to be deeper at the shore at high tide, then goes down again six hours later to low tide.

Right **Snow and rain in the mountains fill the rivers and lakes, which pour into the seas and oceans below.**
Right Inset **The ocean's power reminds us of God's power.**

BEACHES

I made the sand a boundary for the sea, an everlasting barrier it cannot cross. The waves may roll, but they cannot prevail; they may roar, but they cannot cross it. Jeremiah 5:22b

As the ocean washes over shallow places near the land, waves rise up. Waves are great! People swim and surf in them. Waves make sand by crashing against rocks. They also break up millions of little seashells into sand. Without waves there would be no beaches, and no sand castles!

Most waves are gentle, but there are huge waves caused by undersea earthquakes or volcanic eruptions. These are called *tidal waves*, or *tsunamis*. Tsunamis can travel at speeds up to 500 miles per hour and wipe out entire towns.

Above Many creatures live in the cracks and hollows of rocks at the edge of the sea, including sea stars and flowerlike anemones.

As the waters of the sea drop away during low tide each day, pools of water are left behind in the rocks. These little ponds, called *tidal pools,* are filled with wonderful things. Hermit crabs scamper across lawns of seaweed, while sea stars and tiny fish play among the flowerlike sea anemones and spiny purple sea urchins.

Another tidal pool creature is the barnacle. Barnacles are tiny, volcano-shaped shells. When the rocks along the shore are out of the water at low tide, two little doors on top of the shell are closed tight. When the tide comes back up and the rocks are under water, the barnacles open their doors and out pop five or six pairs of things that look like bright feathers. These are actually legs! Barnacles live upside down, waving their legs through the water, scooping up food. These are just a few of the weird and wonderful creatures that our creative God has put at the edge of the sea.

Left Without waves crashing on the shore, there would be no sand for sand castles.

SEAS OF THE BIBLE

I will establish your borders from the Red Sea to the Sea of the Philistines, and from the desert to the River. Exodus 23:31

Many seas are famous because of Bible stories about them. Moses parted the Red Sea so the Israelites could escape from Pharaoh's army. Jesus performed miracles at the Sea of Galilee, and other seas are mentioned in the Bible, too.

One of the seas talked

Above Left **The Sea of Galilee, near Capernaum.**
Above Right **The shore of the Mediterranean Sea.**

about in the Bible is called the *Great Sea*. Today, we know it as the Mediterranean Sea. The Mediterranean, bordered by Europe, Asia, and Africa, was the sea that tied together all of the known world in Bible times.

The Dead Sea was also important in ancient times. The Bible calls it the Salt Sea, and for good reason. The Dead Sea has so much salt that people came great distances to get salt from its shores. It is only forty-five miles long and ten miles across.

One of the most important Bible discoveries was made in a cave next to the Dead Sea. While hiking in the hills, a shepherd boy threw a rock into a cave. He heard the sound of breaking pottery. He climbed inside and found a huge clay jar. When scientists went to the cave, they discovered many jars filled with very old copies of the Old Testament. They were hidden there more than a hundred years before Jesus. The oldest known copy of the Book of Isaiah was there, along with other important scrolls, or ancient books, which have helped us to know more about the Bible and its people.

The Red Sea is the place where one of God's greatest miracles happened. It was there that God used Moses to part the sea while Pharaoh's army was chasing God's people. This provided an escape route. Moses and the Israelites crossed "on dry land" and made

it to the far shore before the sea covered Pharaoh's army.

Perhaps the most important sea in the time of Jesus was the Sea of Galilee. Luke calls this small sea the Lake of Gennesaret. Perhaps "lake" describes it better than sea, because it is smaller than any of the Great Lakes of North America. Nine towns were built on its busy shores. Storms come to the Sea of Galilee almost without warning. It was on this sea that Peter saw Jesus walking on the water, and Jesus calmed the waves of a storm while sailing with His disciples in a boat.

Above **On the Sea of Galilee, Jesus performed a miracle to strengthen Peter's faith.**

RIVERS OF THE WORLD

Above **Even small rivers and streams bring life to the landscape.**

Swarms of living creatures will live wherever the river flows.
Ezekiel 47:9a

Rivers are one way that God gets water to places where there is little rain. People in ancient times liked to live near rivers. They got drinking water from rivers, as well as water for cooking and washing.

Rivers make it easy to travel. Just grab your boat and hop in! We can use rivers to bring boats full of supplies and goods to cities and towns far from the ocean. Rivers have fish to eat, and the soil along them is usually good for farming. In dry areas, farmers dig ditches to bring the water from the rivers to the crops. This is called *irrigation.*

In many parts of the world, people actually live on rivers, building their houses on boats. In China, these boats are called *junks.* Many junks and other boats travel up and down the Yangtze River, the biggest river in Asia.

The longest river in the world is the Nile River in Africa. It's over 4,000 miles long! The widest river is the Mississippi in the United States. Over 250 smaller rivers flow into it from mountain ranges far away. These smaller rivers are called *tributaries.*

Another very important river is the Amazon in South America. Many Indian tribes live along the Amazon River in the dense tropical rain forest. The river and the jungle along it make a home for countless birds and animals. The Amazon is named after female warriors from Greek legends. It was named by a Spanish explorer who saw Indian women warriors on the banks of the river.

Right **The Yangtze River is in China. Chinese boats called "junks" travel up and down the river by towers of rock.**
Right Inset **If we build dams in rivers, like the Hoover Dam near Las Vegas, the power of the river's current can make electricity. But dams also change the plant and animal life along the river.**

RIVERS OF THE BIBLE —THE JORDAN

Then Jesus came from Galilee to the Jordan to be baptized by John. Matthew 3:13

Above **The Jordan River brings life to the valley around it. This is where Jesus and many others were baptized.**
Right **The Jordan parted as the priests crossed with the ark.**
Right Inset **In many places in Bible lands, rivers are dry most of the year.**

Many rivers in Bible lands are small streams that dry up in the summertime. But the Jordan is a big river that flows all year. During the summer, it is very shallow, but in the rainy part of the year it is deeper than a person. The river pours out of the Sea of Galilee and winds its way down to the Dead Sea. From the air, the Jordan looks like a zigzagging snake, turning this way and that across the rugged land.

In many ways, the Jordan reminds us of God's love for His people. God parted the waters of the Jordan for the priests to carry the ark across (Joshua 3). This reminded Joshua and the Israelites of the parting of the Red Sea, and of how powerful and loving their God was.

The people of God camped along the Jordan before going into battle against their enemies, and they stayed at the Jordan when they were getting ready to fight the battle of Jericho. It was the Jordan River that God's people crossed to get to the Promised Land.

Elisha began his ministry at the Jordan by striking it with Elijah's cloak, causing it to part (2 Kings 2), and later he sent Naaman to dip seven times in the waters of the Jordan to be healed of leprosy (2 Kings 5).

John the Baptist used the river to baptize people as a sign of the covenant—or agreement—between God and His people. People were baptized in the water to show God's power in their lives. Even Jesus came to be baptized in the Jordan at the beginning of His ministry. The waters of the Jordan showed people how God could wash away their sin.

THE EUPHRATES, THE TIGRIS, AND THE NILE

The name of the third river is the Tigris; it runs along the east side of Asshur. And the fourth river is the Euphrates. Genesis 2:14

In a hot, dry place called Chaldea, the rain falls for only a few days in winter. The rest of the year it is hot, windy, and dry. Chaldea should be a desert, but God has given it a special gift. High in the mountains, ice melts into dozens of little streams that meet in pools, then lakes. From the lakes, rivers tumble down in magnificent waterfalls, turning into a wide, lazy waterway. A smaller, deeper river comes to meet the slow one, making it even wider. The rivers are the Euphrates and Tigris, and where they meet, the first towns and villages of the world were made.

Above **The ancient city of Ur, built near the Euphrates River.**

These river valleys were home to the Sumerians and later, the Babylonians. The river peoples built cities with canals and giant temples. The ancient Babylonian city of Ur was Abraham's home. Since no trees grew there that could be used for lumber, the Babylonians made their boats out of the reeds that grew along the rivers.

Another important river in Bible times was the Nile. The Nile made it possible for the Egyptians to build their great cities. It made the soil rich and provided a way to get wood, food, and even the great stones used for making the pyramids where they needed to be. At the mouth of the Nile, the Ptolemies of Egypt built the biggest lighthouse ever. It was called the Pharos lighthouse and was one of the seven wonders of the ancient world. As tall as a thirty-story building, it towered over the harbor of Alexandria.

Right **The Pharos lighthouse was built by the Ptolemies of Egypt. Instead of warning ships away from rocks, as today's lighthouses do, it was made to show them the way to the harbor.**

WATERFALLS

He . . . who calls for the waters of the sea and pours them out over the face of the land—the LORD *is his name.* Amos 5:8

The water in a river slowly wears away the rocks it flows over. Some kinds of rock are softer than others. When the soft rock is worn away a hard rock cliff is left, making a waterfall. Niagara Falls is one of the most famous falls in the world. Each minute, 450,000 tons of water pour down the cliffs into a raging river. People can watch the falls from special towers or take boat rides near them. But no swimming—the waterfall is 193 feet tall!

Other famous waterfalls are Victoria Falls in Africa, France's majestic Gavarnie, and California's Yosemite Falls. In South America, Iguacú Falls is nearly two miles across! The tallest waterfall in the world is Angel Falls in Venezuela. It's 3,212 feet tall, a thousand feet taller than any other in the world. It was discovered from an airplane in 1935 by a pilot named James Angel.

The country with the most waterfalls is probably the small island nation of Iceland. Iceland's many glaciers feed hundreds of rivers, and many of those rivers pour over spectacular cliffs made of lava rock. Most of Iceland's energy comes from hydroelectric (water) power.

Waterfalls all over the world come in many shapes and sizes. Here are a few so you can compare them side by side.

Left **Niagara Falls is an enormous waterfall on the border between the United States and Canada. Each second, water as heavy as 450,000 cars pours over its edge.**

Left Inset **A beautiful waterfall in Iceland. The water in this river comes from a melted glacier.**

| Angel Falls (Venezuela) | King George VI (Guyana) | Yosemite Upper Falls (USA) | Gersoppa (India) | Victoria (Rhodesia-Zambia) | Niagara (USA-Canada) |

JONAH AND THE GREAT FISH

There is the sea, vast and spacious, teeming with creatures beyond number—living things both large and small. Psalm 104:25

A long time ago, a man named Jonah discovered that there are many wondrous and sometimes scary creatures in the sea. God asked Jonah to tell the people in Nineveh about Him. But Jonah was afraid. The Ninevites were the enemies of his people. So Jonah took a ship to Tarshish, as far away as he could get. But you cannot run away from God. A storm overtook the ship, and Jonah was thrown overboard. The Bible says he was swallowed by a "great fish." The fish took him back to Nineveh where God wanted him to be! This story is in the Book of Jonah. The people in Bible times were afraid of the strange creatures that swam in the depths of the sea, calling them "leviathans" and "the monsters of the sea."

Most sea creatures are not sent to swallow us up. Instead, they show us how powerful and creative our God is. There are wonderful whales, giant squids, tiny brightly colored shrimp, and graceful manta rays.

The largest creature that has ever lived on Earth is the blue whale. This gentle giant of the seas can weigh as much as fifteen elephants and travels great distances through every ocean in the world. Playful dolphins are a relative of whales. Whales and dolphins are not fish. They breathe air, not water, and are called *mammals*.

The shark is another strange and wonderful creature. The great white shark is very dangerous, but the gigantic whale shark has no teeth and eats tiny shrimp.

In the deepest part of the ocean, there are even creatures that glow in the dark! The deep-sea angler uses a light to catch fish, and the sea dragon has lights running along its sides, just like an airplane.

Right **God uses many things in our lives to teach us. He even used a giant fish to teach Jonah that God knows best.**

SHIPS IN BIBLE TIMES

They passed ropes under the ship itself to hold it together. Fearing that they would run aground on the sandbars of Syrtis, they lowered the sea anchor and let the ship be driven along.

Acts 27:17

In Bible times, the Israelites were good fishermen, but out on the open seas their ships couldn't hold up. The only fleet of trading ships the Jews ever had was sunk at a place called Ezion Geber. This story is in the Book of 1 Kings.

Some people in Bible times knew how to sail the oceans and seas. The Phoenicians built many ships, and the Philistines came across the oceans from Cyprus, an island in the Mediterranean Sea. The Egyptians had great respect for the seamanship of the Minoans, who they called the Sea Peoples. But even to seafarers like the Romans and Greeks, it was too dangerous to travel by sea during the stormy part of the year. Ships stayed home from November to March.

The Apostle Paul found out how dangerous the sea could be. Paul was a prisoner on a grain ship headed for Rome when it was caught in a storm. To try to save the boat, the crew threw the cargo into the raging sea, lowered the big sail, and even wrapped ropes around the boat to keep it from breaking apart. But the ship crashed on a ridge of sand and fell apart. No one died in the storm, and Paul had the chance to tell the people on board all about the love of God.

Above Paul's ship carried 276 people and was as long as ten cars, but it was tiny compared to today's aircraft carriers, which carry 6,000 people.

Right The Apostle Paul was on a big ship when it sank in a storm. This gave Paul a chance to tell his shipmates about God.

TAKING CARE OF OUR RIVERS AND OCEANS

Because of this the land mourns, and all who live in it waste away; the beasts of the field and the birds of the air and the fish of sea are dying. Hosea 4:3

Above **One way to keep our world clean is by using solar energy. Here, the Solar One power station glows white-hot as hundreds of mirrors focus sunlight onto the top of a tower. This heat is turned into electricity with no pollution.**

In the very beginning of the Bible, God tells Adam to care for the Garden of Eden. The Book of Genesis says, "Now the Lord God had planted a garden in the east, in Eden; and there he put the man he had formed" (Genesis 2:8). Ever since Adam, God has called humans to care for His "garden," the Earth. Do you think we are doing a good job?

Plants in the oceans make most of the fresh air that we breathe. The oceans feed us, and the oceans give us salt and minerals, chemicals, and other important things that we use to make our lives better. But we pay the oceans back by throwing garbage into our rivers and streams, dumping chemicals into the seas, and spreading oil across our beautiful beaches and waves. The creatures God has made are getting sick and even dying because of the things we put into the water.

With God, there is always hope. And there is a lot that we can do, too. If you see someone throwing trash into a river or lake, help him or her to see that this is not a good thing to do. Always remember to put your trash where it belongs. Never pour paint or gasoline or other chemicals down your drain if you can help it. The local gas station or recycling station usually has places to dispose of these kinds of liquids.

The sea horses and dolphins God has put in the sea cannot ask us for help. The penguins and sea stars cannot tell us when their homes are being ruined by our thoughtlessness. But each of us can do our part. With God's help, we can all work together to obey His command to care for the Earth.

Above **Ever since the Garden of Eden, God has wanted us to take care of our world and the creatures in it.**
Inset **When we look at the Earth from space, we can see that most of it is covered by oceans, seas, and lakes.**

THE LAST SEA

Also before the throne there was what looked like a sea of glass, clear as crystal. Revelation 4:6

The very last book of the Bible is the strange and wonderful Book of Revelation. It tells us about heaven, about God's plan for good and evil, and about the end of time. In Revelation, we are told about a "glassy sea" in front of the throne of God and four living creatures beside it. Even heaven has a sea!

In ancient times, the people of God made a temple to God. The temple was a model to remind them of what heaven would be like. In this temple was a gigantic bronze bowl on the backs of twelve statues of bulls. This bowl was so big that it was called "the sea" or the "molten sea." When people who had been in the temple heard Revelation, they would remember the giant bowl, a sort of earthly picture of what was to be in heaven.

Above **The peanut-shaped island of Patmos, where the Apostle John saw the Revelation, lies in the Aegean Sea.**

The Bible also tells about a river in heaven. "Then the angel showed me the river of the water of life, as clear as crystal, flowing from the throne of God . . . down the middle of the great street of the city" (Revelation 22:1-2). Did you notice how clear the water in heaven's sea and river is? God has always used water to remind us of how clean He can make us, no matter how messy our lives get! Whenever you look at the great oceans or a thundering waterfall, or even a gurgling stream, remember the great Creator Who made this special part of His creation.

Right **The Bible tells of the beautiful River of Life in heaven. Water has always been a picture God uses to show us how Jesus can wash away the wrong things we do.**